YUVAL ZOMMER

THE BIG STICKER BOOK OF BUGS

Thames & Hudson

This book belongs to:

Illustrated by
YUVAL ZOMMER

First published in the United Kingdom in 2017
by Thames & Hudson Ltd, 181A High Holborn, London
WC1V 7QX

Reprinted 2018

The Big Sticker Book of Bugs © 2017 and 2018 Yuval Zommer

British Library Cataloguing-in-Publication Data
A catalogue record for this book is available
from the British Library

ISBN 978-0-500-65134-6

Printed and bound in China by Everbest Printing Co. Ltd

To find out about all our publications,
please visit **www.thamesandhudson.com**.
There you can subscribe to our e-newsletter,
browse or download our current catalogue,
and buy any titles that are in print.

Hello!

I am your guide, Superfly Freddie.
Follow me through the super-sticky
world of BUGS.

You will need: a pencil, some colouring
pens, and a BUZZING imagination.
You can also get creative with the bug-tastic
stickers at the back of this book.

Let's go!

Stick shells on the backs of these snails. Without shells, snails risk getting eaten by birds!

Draw slimy trails behind
these snails to show
where they have been
in the garden.

Butterflies fly from flower to flower drinking a sweet juice called

Trace this butterfly's
journey around the garden.
Stick butterflies on
every flower it visits.

Butterflies flap their wings to fly.
Design new wings for these butterflies.

Ants live in nests where they store their food.
Stick ants in the nest to create a single line
from the strawberry patch to the food store.

Food Store

Strawberry Patch

Some bugs can swim underwater.
Stick pond bugs in this pond.
Are they swimming backstroke
or front crawl?

Draw algae for these bugs
to hide behind to keep
them safe from fish.

Which bugs are making
this garden glow at night?
Hint: they look like flying
worms with glowing tails.

Centipedes can have between about 30 and 300 legs! Draw legs on these centipedes to help them move.

 Dragonflies are fast and furious at flying. Stick dragonflies in the air and make them do loop-the-loop!

Baby dragonflies are born
in the water from eggs.
Draw wings on these
nymphs so they can
join in the flying fun.

Ladybirds love eating tiny
green bugs called aphids.
Stick ladybirds on the leaves
to gobble up the aphids.

A ladybird's bright wings warn
birds that they are poisonous.
Colour this ladybird bright red
or orange to warn off the birds.

Did you know ladybirds have been taken up to space in a rocket to help space scientists with their research?

Design your own spacecraft.
Draw some adventurous
ladybirds inside.

A grasshopper has short feelers.
A cricket has long feelers.
Spot the odd bug out!

Play Grasshoppers and Crickets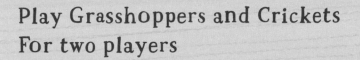
For two players

How to Play:
Use grasshopper and cricket
stickers from the back of the
book. Choose between you who
will take which bug. Take turns
placing a bug on the grid.
The first player to get three
bugs in a row wins!

Beetles have hard shells
to keep their wings safe.
Colour in the shells of
these beetles.

Stick beetles in this woodland setting.

Flies love a good picnic
just as much as we do!
Draw your favourite picnic
food on the plates.

Stick flies on the food
that you think they'll
enjoy most.

A spider pulls a strong thread
of silk out of its body.
It spins a web of silk to
catch bugs for its dinner.

Stick flies in the web to
feed this hungry spider.

Earthworms dig tunnels
that let air into the soil.
The air helps plants to grow.

Stick worms in the soil
so these veggies grow
even bigger.

Play Bugs in a Rug
For two players

How to play:
Take turns drawing one line at a time between
the white dots (no diagonal lines are allowed).
When you complete a square, write your initials
inside it. The player with the most squares wins!

The Lifecycle of a Butterfly

Use the stickers from the back of the book to complete this picture.

1. Caterpillar
A butterfly starts life as
a tiny egg that hatches
into a caterpillar.

2. Chrysalis
The caterpillar makes a
shell called a chrysalis.
Inside, it starts to change.

3. Butterfly
The shell splits open.
The caterpillar has
turned into a butterfly.

Who has been eating these leaves? Find the most likely suspects and stick them on the leaves.

 Termites build towers taller than a person out of soil, spit, wood and poo!

Design a termite tower.
Stick termites all over it.

These buzzing bees are
busy collecting nectar
to make honey.

Which worker bee
visited which flower?
Follow the lines to
find out the answe

 Inside the beehive is where bees store honey.
Stick bees on the honeycomb and imagine
the honey flowing...

The bees have turned their
nectar into honey and it is ready
for the beekeeper to collect.
Design your own honey jar label.

Stick spiders on the ends of
these long threads of silk.

Which spider is closest
to catching the fly?

Stick insects look like
sticks so bigger animals
don't try to eat them.
Circle the stick insects
in this picture. Can you
spot the leaf insect too?

Draw legs, eyes and feelers on this
stick to make it look like an insect.

Do the same for this leaf!

Test Your Bug Knowledge

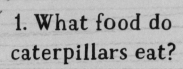

1. What food do caterpillars eat?

2. Where do bees store their honey?

3. What do spiders catch in their web?

4. Do grasshoppers have short feelers or long feelers?

5. Where do worms live?

Check your answers below to find out if you are a bug expert!

Butterflies

Ants

Pond Bugs

Glow Worms

Dragonflies

Ladybirds

Grasshoppers
& Crickets

Beetles

Flies

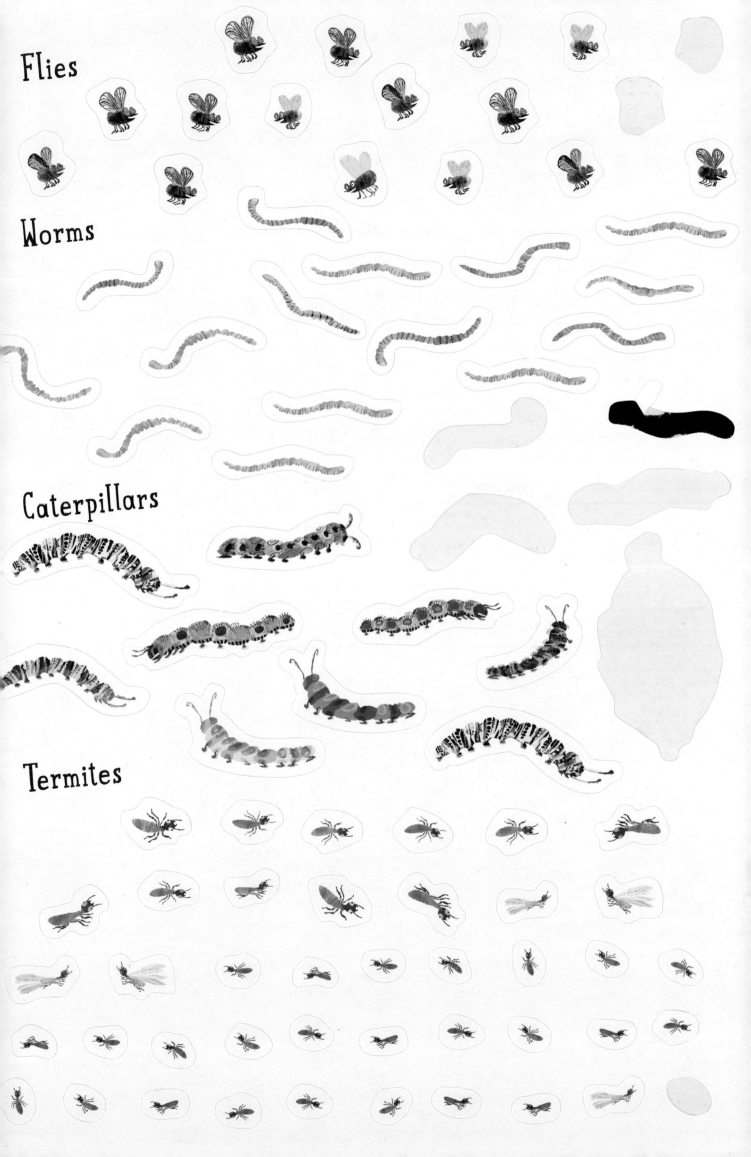

Flies

Worms

Caterpillars

Termites

Bees

Spiders

Snails